W9-CDW-313

The Little Witch's Thanksgiving Book

by Linda Glovach

Prentice-Hall, Inc., Englewood Cliffs, New Jersey

Printed in the United State of America   .J

Prentice-Hall International, Inc., London
Prentice-Hall of Australia, Pty. Ltd.,
    North Sydney
Prentice-Hall of Canada, Ltd., Toronto
Prentice-Hall of India Private Ltd., New Delhi
Prentice-Hall of Japan, Inc., Tokyo

10 9 8 7 6 5 4 3 2 1

Library of Congress Cataloging in Publication
    Data

Glovach, Linda.
    The Little Witch's Thanksgiving book.

    Includes index.
    SUMMARY: Handicrafts, a puppet play, and
recipes related to the celebration of Thanksgiving Day.
    1. Handicraft—Juvenile literature.
2. Cookery—Juvenile literature. 3. Thanksgiving Day—Juvenile literature. [1. Thanksgiving Day. 2. Handicraft. 3. Cookery.
4. Puppets and puppet-plays] I. Title.
TT160.G55   745.59'41   76-9847
ISBN 0-13-537993-8

For Jannine and Peter

TABLE OF CONTENTS

THE STORY
OF THANKSGIVING:
Thanksgiving Plays
and Puppets

The Story of Thanksgiving

More than 300 years ago a group of Pilgrims decided to leave their homes in England and go to America. They were hoping to find more freedom and perhaps a better way of life there.

The Little Witch and her friends make their Pilgrim and Indian costumes (page 12 through 15) and act out the Story of Thanksgiving.

One cold morning in September the Pilgrims set sail from Plymouth, England, on the ship *Mayflower*, with 102 passengers. The ship was crowded, and the journey long and cold. The people were hungry and tired.

Finally they pulled into a harbor. Miles Standish and his men stepped on shore first to see if it was safe. The land was filled with thickets and thorns, and they had heard about Indians that might not be friendly. The rest of the Pilgrims came ashore and wandered about. The Indians watched all this from a distance. Then one of the Pilgrims dug up some of the Indians' corn.

The Indians shot at them with their bows and arrows. The Pilgrims shot back with their guns.

When things calmed down, the Pilgrims returned to their ship and sailed across the bay to another area they found on the map, Plymouth Rock, Massachusetts.

There they found trees and fresh water, the land was already cleared and the soil looked good for planting. The Indians were already living there.

In the middle of winter, the Pilgrims began building their homes. It was bitter cold and the ground was frozen. Many of the Pilgrims became sick and died.

The Indians who lived there did not trust the Pilgrims at first, so they stayed in the distance.

Then one day in March, when the winter had passed, an Indian named Samoset walked into the Pilgrims' village. He spoke about many matters. When he left they had become friends.

A short time later, more Indians came into the village, led by their Chief Massasoit. The Pilgrims welcomed them into a cabin and gave them beads and something to eat. They talked for many hours and became very good friends.

Squanto, another Indian who spoke English, stayed behind to live with the Pilgrims. He showed them how to grow corn and other vegetables and how to live off the land.

By the time autumn came, a beautiful harvest of corn and crops had come up. The Pilgrims were so grateful that they decided to have a feast on a special day to celebrate all they had to be thankful for. They called it Thanksgiving Day, and they invited the Indians, for without their help the Pilgrims might have starved.

Today, people in many lands still celebrate Thanksgiving every year on the fourth Thursday of November.

MAKE COSTUMES

Pilgrim Woman

You need: 12″ X 18″ and 20″ X 32″ pieces of crepe paper; 4 ribbons, each 10″ long; long skirt; white blouse; stapler; scissors.

FLUFF RIM OUT

FRONT CORNER

FOLD BACK CORNERS around TO MEET front CORNERS

CAPE

Fold 12″ X 18″ crepe paper 4″ down from the top. Turn top corners in and staple down. Push the rim out. Bring back corners around to meet front corners so sides of bonnet fold like a fan and fluff out like a bonnet. Hold in place and staple front and back corners together on each side.

Staple 1½″ of a ribbon to each corner and tie the ribbons under your chin.

To make a cape, staple 1½″ of the end of a ribbon to each top corner of the black crepe paper. Wear it over your shoulders and tie ribbons around your chest. Wear a long skirt and white blouse. To see final costume, see pictures on pages 9 through 11.

Pilgrim Man

You need: 12″ X 14″ piece of black construction paper; 2½″ X 3″ piece of yellow construction paper; oatmeal box; 2 strings, each 12″ long; 6½″ X 7″ piece of crepe paper for beard; 20″ X 32″ piece of black crepe paper; 2 ribbons, each 10″ long; stapler, scissors; paints; tights, pants and shirt; 2 large rubber bands.

Paint oatmeal box black. Cut a circle out of the 12″ X 14″ paper. Trace the rim of the box in the center of the circle. Cut out inside your lines. Staple an end of a string to each side of the box.

Slip the circle over the box, and push down as hat rim. Cut a yellow buckle out of the yellow paper and glue to the front of the box.

Cut ½″ X 6½″ strips up the 6½″ X 7″ crepe paper. Staple an end of each string to each corner. Pull strings up over ears and tie in back of your head.

TRACE RIM ON CIRCLE —

13

Make cape for Pilgrim man the same as Pilgrim women. Put on tights. Roll your pants up at the knees and hold them in place with a rubber band. Wear your shirt out with a belt around the waist. You can tape hat buckles (page 13) on your shoes if you like.

Indians

You need: 2″ wide strip of construction paper; construction paper for feathers, each 2″ X 8″, 1″ X 6″ strips of construction paper for necklace; tempera paints, pencil, stapler, scissors; clear tape; paper straws; 2″ X 2″ light colored construction paper.

Draw triangles on the 2″ X 2″ pieces of paper. Cut them out and tape straws to the back of each triangle to make arrows.

Wear a long-sleeved polo shirt or plain long-sleeved turtleneck tucked into your pants. Wear pants that are long but tight on you, and a short jacket (suede, if you have one) if you play outdoors.

Measure around your head and cut a 2″ wide piece of construction paper that length with 2″ left over. Paint and decorate it. Fit it around your head, overlap 1″ of ends and staple closed. Draw leaf shapes on the 2″ X 8″ pieces and cut them out. Cut triangular slits into the paper to make them look like feathers. Staple the feathers in place on the headband. For an Indian chief, make more feathers around the sides and back of the band.

Put rouge on your face for war paint. Make a chain necklace like the one on this page, using 1″ X 6″ strips and making it long enough to hang around your neck.

Thanksgiving Sock Puppet Play

You can have a Thanksgiving puppet play at home or in school. The play on page 23 is the Little Witch's version of the First Thanksgiving Feast. She makes her puppets out of socks and simple materials. Get your friends together and choose the characters you want to be. You need each other's help to make the puppets. While one person is wearing the sock, the other person can fit the costume on it.

Here is how to use the sock:

Put the sock over your hand as shown in the picture and bend your fingers. Move your fingers up and down to make the puppet talk.

Pilgrim Women, Priscilla and Mary

You need: A white sock; colored crepe paper, 4" X 7"; crepe paper, 3" X 8" (use a different color for each puppet); 4 pieces of ribbon, each 5"; tempera paints; scissors; glue.

Put sock on your hand and paint a woman's face as shown in the picture. Cut a triangle out of the width of the 4" X 7" crepe paper. Make a hole in 1" from each corner. Tie a ribbon end through each hole. While you wear the sock, have a helper wrap the crepe paper around sock to fit as a bonnet. Put a dab of glue on the bonnet to hold it to the sock. Tie the ribbons under the chin. Glue small strips of crepe paper to the top rim of the bonnet for hair. Put glue on the point of the bonnet in the back and glue it to the sock.

Attach a ribbon to each top corner of the 3" X 8" crepe paper. Have a helper wrap crepe paper around your wrist for a cape and tie the ribbons. Paint on buttons if you like.

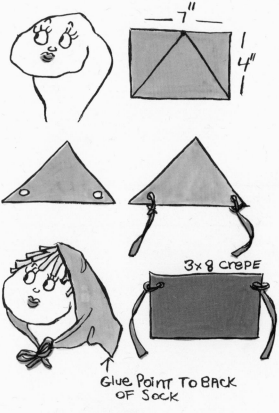

3x8 crepe

Glue Point To BACK OF Sock

Pilgrim Men, Miles Standish, John Hopkins

For each you need: a white sock; a 3 oz. paper cup painted black; 3½″ X 4″ piece of black construction paper; tiny strips of crepe paper for beard and hair, ⅜″ X 2½″; 3″ X 8″ piece of black crepe paper; 2 ribbons, each 5″ long; tempera paints, scissors, glue, stapler.

TRACE RIM ON CIRCLE

CUT INSIDE LINES

Put sock on and paint a man's face on it. Cut several ⅜″ X 2½″ strips and glue to chin as beard, and to sides and back of sock as hair.

Cut a circle out of the black paper. Trace the rim of the cup in the middle of the circle. Cut out inside your lines. Slip the circle over the cup to make a hat rim. Cut little slits at the bottom of cup. Bend and staple to the rim if the rim slips off the cup.

Make a cape of the 3″ X 8″ crepe paper same as woman (page 12).

18

Indians, Samoset, Chief Massasoit

For each you need: a reddish or light brown sock; 3½″ X 4″ piece of black crepe paper; 2 pieces of colored construction paper, each 1″ X 3″; tempera paints, scissors, glue; strips of ½″ X 3″ construction paper.

Paint an Indian face and warpaint on the sock. Fold the width of the crepe paper in half. Cut 1½″ strips up the opened end. Bend the top fold down. Make a sharp crease. Glue folded part to top and down the back of sock, fluff out the fringe.

Draw leaves on the construction paper. Draw triangular slits and cut out on your lines, to make feathers. Cut a point at the bottom. Bend the bottom and glue it to the hair on the back of the sock.

Make a necklace for Chief Massasoit. Fold a strip in a circle and glue it closed. Put another strip through it and glue it closed. Continue until necklace is long enough to slip over the sock. Glue ends closed.

Turkey

You need: light brown sock; 1½″ X 3″ yellow construction paper; cotton; 4″ diameter circle of brown construction paper; 3″ X 8″ brown crepe paper; 2 pieces of string, each 5″ long; tempera paints; scissors; glue.

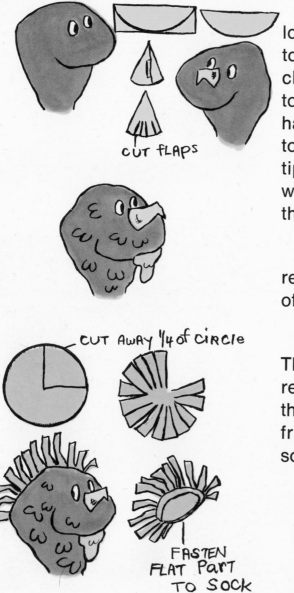

CUT FLAPS

CUT AWAY ¼ of CiRCle

FASTEN FLAT PaRT TO SOCK

Draw a half-circle on the yellow paper. Cut it out. Turn it to form a cone. Tape seams closed. Cut little slits in the bottom edge. Put the sock on your hand. Have a helper glue flaps to the sock as a beak. Bend the tip down to form a hook. Paint white and black markings on the sock for feathers.

Paint a small dab of cotton red and glue it under the chin of the turkey.

Cut ¼ of the 4″ circle away. Then cut 1½″ strips around rest of the circle. Bend back the strips and glue the unfringed area to the back of the sock as head feathers.

Draw curved lines on the crepe paper to form wings. Paint white markings for feathers. Cut out on the lines. Staple the strings to the top corners. Tie the strings around the neck (your wrist) as wings.

Narrator

The narrator is made like a Pilgrim woman. Give her different color hair, bonnet, and cape from Priscilla and Mary.

Make and Decorate the Stage

You need: long grocery carton, large enough for six puppets with background space; paints; scissors.

Set carton up so long side is your theater. Have an adult cut away top and bottom. Then cut ¾ of the side away to make a frame, as shown in picture.

Bend flaps to loosen them. Paint scenery on each flap: a blue sky, trees, cabins, with some water in the distance. Paint cornstalks and leaves, and some birds in the sky.

—narrator

CUT AWAY TO MAKE FRAME

Cover a table with some sheets and set your stage on it. The puppet players stay hidden behind the table except when they are on stage.

PROPS

Thanksgiving Dinner Table (for Act Two)
You need: long narrow cardboard box to fit on stage, or 4″ X 8″ cardboard and four 1″ X 2″ pieces for legs.

Cut legs out of the bottom of the box and stand it up. If you are making your own table, bend the tips of the four strips and glue them to the 4″ X 8″ piece. Paint the table brown and put a napkin or hanky over it.

Food for Feast (for Act Two)
First scatter some corn kernels over the floor of your stage. A plastic pumpkin is nice, too. Prepare some berries, small nuts, and raisins. Put them in doll dishes on the dinner table.

Keep a record player handy to play music for the Indian Dance.

A Puppet Play
THE THANKSGIVNG FEAST

Characters

Miles Standish—a Pilgrim man
John Hopkins—a Pilgrim man
Priscilla—a Pilgrim woman
Mary—a younger Pilgrim woman
Samoset—an Indian man
Chief Massasoit—an Indian chief
Setting: Plymouth, Massachusetts

ACT I

Narrator: The Pilgrims worked hard all year with the help of the Indians to grow their crops. Now it was autumn and a beautiful harvest had come up.

[Miles, John, Priscilla, and Mary on stage.]

Miles: (admiring the crops) Let us be thankful for all that we have. Our crops have grown tall, and there is enough food for winter.

John: Yes, and we must never forget the Indians for the help they have given us.

Miles: I would like to declare a special feast, for men, women, and children to celebrate our good fortune in this new land.

TURKEY
GOBBLE GOBBLE

Priscilla: That is a wonderful idea! Some of the women can cook and bake the food. What a delicious feast it will be!

Mary: We will have it outdoors, and invite Chief Massasoit and his people. Oh, I can almost taste the pumpkin pie!

Miles: I'll go and invite the Indians now. We will have it in three days, and call it a Thanksgiving Day Feast.

John: I'll gather the men to hunt for deer and wild turkey.

[Men go off stage; women talk while hurrying off stage.]

Priscilla: We must run and tell the women to begin preparing the food. We only have a few days.

Mary: I hope we have enough molasses for the pumpkin pie.

[Turkey comes on stage, singing to himself.]

Turkey: Dum de dum, ra-ta-ta-tum, what a wonderful day, not too hot, not too cold, perfect for snoozing.

[John comes up quietly from the back, sees turkey.]

John: A wild turkey! Just what I've been looking for, perfect for the Thanksgiving Feast.

[John chases turkey, catches him. Both go off stage.]

ACT II

Narrator: The day of the feast has arrived. The women are busy setting the tables.

[Narrator goes off stage. Priscilla and Mary enter, put table and food on stage. Miles, John, Mary, and Priscilla sit at the table. Turkey puts his head on the table (he is cooked). Massasoit and Samoset enter. Miles and John stand up to greet them.]

Miles: Welcome, Chief Massasoit and Samoset. Please come and join us.

Samoset: [giving Pilgrims a food gift; you can use a small cookie] Here is a token of our friendship. [Everyone sits down.]

Miles: We thank you very much.

[Narrator enters.]

Narrator: The rest of the Indians came shortly. They sat at long tables like this one or on the ground with the rest of the Pilgrims. There was plenty of food for all.

Miles: [bowing his head in prayer] Let us be thankful for the food before us, and our new home, and our friends.

Samoset: And let us be thankful for the trees, the rivers, the sun, and the food that grows from the earth.

[Audience can repeat prayer with Samoset. All characters eat and enjoy feast. Play music, Indians do a dance.]

Narrator: The feast lasted three days. The cold winter would come again, and there would be lots of work to do, but this day was never forgotten, and we still celebrate Thanksgiving Day every autumn in November.

A Thanksgiving Day Recipe

The Pilgrims made bread out of their corn, and they served it at the Thanksgiving celebration.

You can make some cornbread before the play. Cut it in small slices and serve it to your audience, after the play, so they can join in the Thanksgiving Feast. Here is an old-fashioned recipe. Serve it with apple juice in paper cups, if you like.

PILGRIM'S CORNBREAD

2 cups cornmeal
2 tsps. baking powder
1 egg, beaten

1 cup milk
2 tbsps. oil
2 tbsps. sugar
½ tsp. salt

Sift together dry ingredients. Add milk, oil, egg, and sugar. Mix well. Pour batter into a greased, 8″ square pan. Bake in a preheated oven at 400° for 35 minutes.

Thanksgiving Outdoors

Thanksgiving is the time of the harvest when the crops grown in the previous months are ripe and ready to pick.

You can make many colorful decorations and tasty foods to eat from the things that grow outdoors. The little witch starts by collecting leaves in her backyard.

Pressing Leaves

The prettiest leaves fall in autumn. The little witch gathers the ones that are the most colorful.

You need: leaves that are flat, a little damp, not torn, and have their stems; heavy books.

Dry your leaves three weeks before Thanksgiving.

Put the leaves between the pages of heavy books. Do not put more than one leaf on a page. Lay the books flat and put other heavy books over them as weights.

When they are thoroughly dry, you are ready to make some decorations.

If you don't like the colors of your leaves, you can paint them harvest colors of orange, yellow, red, or brown with tempera paints.

Paint both sides of the leaves. You can make many interesting designs with your leaves by arranging them on different shapes of construction paper.

Draw a tree on 12″ X 18″ brown construction paper and staple leaves on the branches. Hang it up. Paste some acorns on, too. Paint the bark on the tree. Make smaller and bigger trees if you like.

Cover a small milk container with crepe paper to be a vase. Put some painted leaves in the spout. You can put your leaves in jars, bottles, or under glass.

Draw a big round pumpkin with a stem. Staple two leaves at the base of the stem. Tie a string through the stem. Hang it up.

PAINT DESIGNS ON PAPER

APPLE DOLLS

Apples are fun to eat, but did you know that the early settlers, who did not have modern toys, made dolls out of them? Here are the little witch's directions to make a special Apple Witch Doll. You will need an adult to help you.

You need: small apple; knife; 2" dowel or piece of a pencil; 4 pipe cleaners; several 1" X 12" strips of crepe paper; glue; scissors; navy beans; rouge; varnish; paints; one-half of a 6" diameter circle of black construction paper; 3" diameter circle of black construction paper; 2 pieces of string, each 5" long; small crepe paper strips for hair; black crepe paper, one piece 10" X 18", and one piece 5" X 4"; 4 strings.

Remove the apple stem. Peel the apple. Scoop a hole at the blossom end, just big enough to slip your dowel or pencil in. Cut out two eyes, carve a witch's nose and make a slit for the mouth. Carve a bumpy chin. The features will look very rough.

Put the apple in a warm place, on top of a water heater or radiator. It takes three to four weeks to dry. As it dries it will shrink and turn brown.

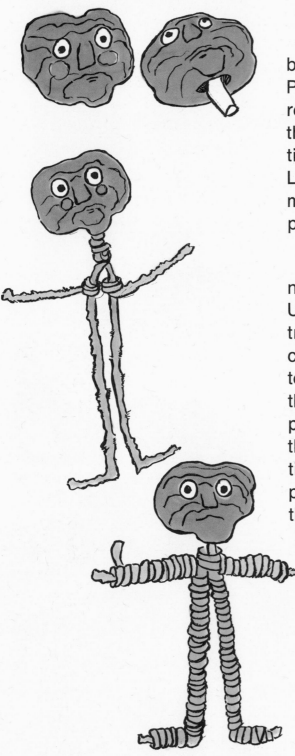

When it is ready, glue navy beans in the holes for eyes. Paint black spots on them. Rub rouge on each cheek. Color the mouth also. Brush the entire head with clear varnish. Let the varnish dry, then cement about ½″ of the dowel or pencil in the head.

Attach pipe cleaners to the neck to start making the body. Use two pipe cleaners for the trunk and legs. Bend pipe cleaners for feet. Attach arms to the trunk. Begin wrapping the crepe paper around the pipe cleaners until it is several thicknesses. Glue each portion down at the end. You may paint the crepe paper to match the face, if you like.

Roll the half-circle into a cone. Tape the ends closed. Trace the rim of cone on center of 3″ circle. Cut out inside your line. Slip the circle over the cone. Tape it in place if it is loose. Staple an end of a string to each side inside of rim. Tape strips of crepe paper to the inside of the rim of the hat on sides and back for hair. Put it on the apple witch's head and tie strings under her chin.

Fold the length of 10″ X 18″ crepe paper in half. Wrap it very loosely around the body of the doll. Tie a string around the waist. Roll a small ball of crepe paper and slip it inside the crepe paper above the string. Tie another string above the ball. Fluff out the skirt by cutting some slits up from the bottom.

Staple an end of each string to a corner of the 5″ X 4″ crepe paper. Put it around the doll's shoulders as a cape. Make it several thicknesses if you want fullness.

TRACE RIM

CREPE HAIR

CAPE

PUT BALL IN HERE

BODY of DOll IS UNDER CREPE

CUT SLITS

33

Drying Corn

The Indians dried their extra corn so they would have it to eat for the rest of the year when the growing season was over. You can dry your corn and eat it. It turns very hard, but it tastes almost like candy. Store it in small glass jars.

You need: small can of corn (7 oz.) or fresh cooked corn scraped from the cob; paper towels; clean jars; wide tray.

Do this on a sunny day. Drain the canned corn, then put it on paper towels to absorb moisture. Then spread corn out evenly on a wide flat tray. Put it in a 350° oven for fifteen minutes.

Take the tray outside and let the corn finish drying in the hot sun. It should take a few hours. When the corn is dry, bring it inside and store it in a jar.

Don't eat it all now. Save some for the rest of the year when Thanksgiving is over.

COUNT THE CORN GAME

Use your dried corn to play this game, when your friends come to visit. Take the corn out of the jar and count how many kernels you have. Write the amount on a piece of paper, then put the corn back in the jar. Don't let anyone see the number you wrote down.

Have your friends sit around a small table. Put the jar of corn in the center of it. Give each person a pencil and paper. Then they have to try to guess, just by looking, how many kernels are in the jar, and write that number on the paper. The winner is the one who comes closest to the number that you wrote down.

Natural Food Recipe

HARVEST BOWL

2 apples
a bunch of grapes
honey

a handful of nuts
2 handfuls of raisins
wheatgerm

Have your mother help you peel, core, and dice the apples. Put them in a bowl. Add the nuts, raisins, and grapes. Mix together well. Add 2 tablespoons (or more if you like) of honey, mix lightly and sprinkle with crunchy wheatgerm. Serve in small bowls to your family and friends.

THANKSGIVING
AT HOME

Real Thanksgiving Pumpkin Pie

The little witch makes her pumpkin pie out of fresh-picked pumpkins like the Pilgrims did. You can use a prepared pie shell, though, because it makes things a lot easier. Mother Witch helps cook the pumpkin. When you go out for your pumpkin, pick a ripe, dark orange pie pumpkin.

EASY PUMPKIN PIE

1¾ cups cooked pumpkin
⅔ cup sugar
2 eggs, beaten
2 cups milk

1 tsp. cinnamon
¼ tsp. nutmeg
1 tsp. salt
¼ tsp. ginger

DISCARD FIBERS

Wash and cut the pumpkin in quarters, discard the seeds and fibers. Place ½" of hot water in a shallow baking pan and bake in a 350° oven for 40 minutes. Cut the pulp of the pumpkin from the rind and mash it up.

Cool the pumpkin in the freezer for a few minutes.

Now, make the pie recipe, using 1¾ cups of your cooked pumpkin. Mix all the ingredients together in a bowl. Pour into a 9″ unbaked pie shell. Bake at 450° for 15 minutes. Then lower the heat to 325° and continue baking for about 30 minutes, or when a knife inserted in the center comes out clean.

If you can't wait until Thanksgiving Day to eat your pie, invite your friends over for an early Thanksgiving treat. It tastes delicious with whipped cream squirted on top, and each friend can squirt their own, provided, of course, they don't make a terrible mess.

SCARECROW CORNHUSK DOLL

The Indian children made dolls out of cornhusks. Today, some children who live in the Appalachian and Ozark Mountains still play with cornhusk dolls. The little witch makes a scarecrow out of cornhusks for her front door.

You need: cornhusks; string; water colors; scissors.

Choose soft cornhusks; usually the inner husks are better. Soak them in warm water until soft, about an hour, then drain on paper towels. Keep husks damp with a cloth or sponge while working with them.

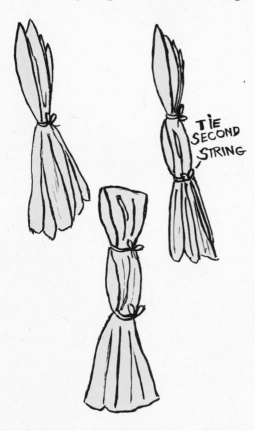

Put 5 or 6 husks together and tie a string around the middle for a waist. Tie another piece of string about 2″ above that for the body. Fold the ends of the husks down from the top and hold them down by tying them in place with a string around the neck.

Put 2 husks together and tie near the ends with strings for arms and hands. Roll and slip the arms through the opening in the top of the body near the neck, or tie the arms to the body by wrapping string around them at the neck.

If you want a lady scarecrow, keep the bottom of the dress as is. For a man, divide or cut the husks below the waist. Roll into trouser leg and fasten with strings at the bottom for feet. Paint a shirt and skirt or pants to look like a scarecrow on the husks with water colors. Paint the face also.

DIVIDE BELOW THE WAIST

Glue strips of crepe paper around the head for hair. Cotton can be used for hair and a beard for an elderly scarecrow. Eyeglasses can be cut out of construction paper and glued on.

CALABASH GOURDS

Calabash gourds are a fruit that grows in many interesting shapes and sizes and can easily be made into dishes, dippers, bottles, jugs, etc. The Indians even made dance rattles and pipes out of them. The early settlers served some of their food in them. The little witch makes a dipper out of her gourd for her Thanksgiving table. It can also be used as a serving dish. Most markets sell calabash gourds.

You need: an adult to help you; a plain, smooth calabash that has a neck that looks like a handle; knife, handsaw; sandpaper.

SAW ONE SIDE

Saw off one side of the gourd. Scrape the inside pulp from the walls of the gourd with a knife. Sandpaper the walls to a smooth surface. Make sure the inside is very clean.

If you like, you can paint designs on the gourd, such as Indian markings. Spray a paint fixitive over it.

The little witch makes cranberry sauce to serve in her gourd for Thanksgiving dinner. You can also use your gourd as a serving dish for anything you like.

CRANBERRY SAUCE
(makes 2 cups)

2 cups water   1 lb. cranberries   2 cups sugar

Combine ingredients in a large saucepan. Heat to boiling, stirring until sugar dissolves. Keep boiling until berries pop open. Turn into a dish. Chill. Serve it in your gourd on Thanksgiving Day.

INDIAN PLACECARDS

The little witch helps with the preparation of the Thanksgiving dinner by making placecards. Be sure to make one for each person who will be sitting at your table.

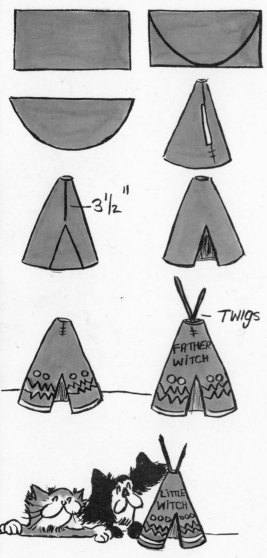

Draw a half-circle, starting from the top corners on the paper. Cut it out and turn it to form a cone shape. Be sure to keep the bottom of the cone even, so that it stands up. Staple and tape the seam closed.

Measure 3½″ down from the top of the cone and draw a triangle for the door. Cut it out. Paint a design on your tepee, leaving a space in the middle to write the name of the person. You can put a small twig or two in the opening at the top of the tepee if you like.

Put the placecards on the table so each person will know where to sit.

PEPPERMINT HERB TEA

After Thanksgiving dinner, the little witch brews tea from the herbs that grow in her garden. She invites her friends over to taste it, with cookies. This recipe will serve 2 adults or 4 children.

You need: dried peppermint leaves; a tea pot; a strainer; honey or sugar. Have your mother help you.

Put 2 cups of water into the teakettle. Bring the water to a boil. Pour half of the water in one cup and half in another. Put 1 teaspoon of dried leaves into each teacup. Let it steep for five minutes.

Strain the tea into fresh cups. To serve your friends, you will need 4 cups. This tea tastes strong, so only give each friend a half-cup of tea. Sweeten with lots of honey, or sugar.

The little witch and her friends dim the lights and sit in the parlor and talk about all the good things they enjoyed for Thanksgiving dinner. One of the little witch's friends tells a funny story he knows about some children who ate too much turkey, pie, and cranberry sauce, and that night while they slept, a giant turkey, pumpkin, and huge cranberry came into their rooms and carried them out of their beds to take them home and eat them! Did this really happen? Maybe they just dreamed it because they were so full.

3